Suspicious Activity Reporting in the Gaming Industry

Based on Filings of Suspicious Activity Reports by Casinos and Card Clubs from January 1, 2004, through June 30, 2011

March 2012

Suspicious Activity Reporting in the Gaming Industry

Based on Filings of Suspicious Activity Reports by Casinos and Card Clubs from January 1, 2004, through June 30, 2011

March 2012

Table of Contents

Executive Summary

Gaming institutions covered by FinCEN's regulations submitted 74,816 Suspicious Activity Report by Casinos and Card Clubs (SAR-C) filings from 2004 through June 2011. Dollar amounts reported in these filings totaled $1.77 billion. Annual filings consistently increased, while total dollar amounts fluctuated from year to year. The steady increase in SAR-C filings during the study period paralleled a significant expansion of gaming operations across the United States.

State-licensed casinos filed about 70 percent of the SAR-Cs and accounted for about 80 percent of the reported dollar amount of suspicious activity. Tribal casinos submitted approximately 26 percent of the filings and accounted for 16 percent of the dollar amount. Card clubs submitted 2 percent of the filings and accounted for 2 percent of the dollar amount.

New Jersey and Nevada are by far the states with the highest number of SAR-C filings. Together, they accounted for 41 percent of all filings over the period and 61 percent of the reported dollar amount. New Jersey casinos filed the highest number of reports, while Nevada casinos reported the highest total dollar amount.

More than 40 percent of the filings reported suspicious activities characterized as structuring. The reports frequently described activities involving chip, jackpot and token redemptions, which customers may have structured to avoid currency transaction reporting requirements.

The second most frequently reported characterization of suspicious activity was "Other." In these SAR-Cs, narratives often described situations in which patrons or employees displayed unusual behavior or violated casino policies. The third most frequent characterization was "Minimal Gaming with Large Transactions." The narratives in these reports described situations in which patrons bought chips or deposited funds into their casino front money accounts and then cashed out after little or no play.

The types of suspicious activities reported reflected known money laundering and criminal techniques. As reports of these activities have increased, casinos have expanded the amount of useful information available to FinCEN and its law enforcement customers seeking to deter and detect criminal abuse of the gaming industry.

Introduction

Casinos and card clubs are vulnerable to money laundering and other financial crimes because of the nature of their operations. These gaming institutions are fast-paced, cash-intensive businesses that often provide a broad array of financial products and services, some of which are similar to those provided by depository institutions and money services businesses. Moreover, gaming institutions serve a diverse and transient customer base about which they may have relatively little knowledge. Casinos became subject to anti-money laundering regulations promulgated under the Bank Secrecy Act (BSA) in 1985.[1]

Since then, gaming operations across the country have greatly expanded. In 1985, only Nevada and New Jersey allowed casino gambling. In 1989, two other states legalized certain types of limited stakes gambling. Over the following decade, a number of other states legalized full-scale casino gambling in riverboat and/or land-based casinos, while Native American tribes began to open casinos on Indian tribal lands. Today, legal forms of gambling (including casinos, card clubs, lotteries, racetracks, and bingo) exist in a majority of the states, as well as in Puerto Rico and the U.S. territories. According to the American Gaming Association (AGA) 2011 survey of casino entertainment, the industry now includes about 438 land-based or riverboat casinos, 45 racetrack casinos, and 510 card rooms, including card rooms located within land-based casinos.[2] As of July 2011, the National Indian Gaming Commission listed 240 Indian tribes with 460 gaming operations across 28 states.[3]

---

1. See Final Rule – Casino Regulations, 50 FR 5065 (February 6, 1985). The rulemaking defined state-licensed casinos as financial institutions. Businesses defined as financial institutions at 31 CFR § 1010.100(t) are required to report transactions in currency and maintain records on transmittals of funds. See 31 CFR §§ 1010.306 -315 and 410. The Money Laundering Suppression Act of 1994 subsequently codified the application of the BSA to gaming activities. See 31 U.S.C. 5312(a)(2)(X). Rules defining tribal casinos and card clubs as financial institutions were issued in 1996 and 1998. See Final Rule –Regulations Regarding Tribal Gaming, 61 FR 7054 (February 23, 1996) and Final Rule – Amendments to Bank Secrecy Act Regulations Regarding Reporting and Recordkeeping by Card Clubs, 63 FR 1919 (January 13, 1998).

2. See the American Gaming Association (AGA) 2011 State of the States Report: The AGA Survey of Casino Entertainment at http://www.americangaming.org/files/aga/uploads/docs/sos/aga-sos-2011.pdf

3. See the National Indian Gaming Commission, Frequently Asked Questions, at http://www.nigc.gov/About_Us/Frequently_Asked_Questions.aspx

---

This report presents an overview of SAR-C filings by casinos and card clubs over the last 7-1/2 years. It includes statistics showing filing volumes, types of gaming institutions submitting SAR-Cs, reported suspicious activity dollar amounts, and characterizations of suspicious activity. The report also lists activities described in a representative selection of SAR-C narratives.

Regulatory Background

The definition of a financial institution at 31 CFR § 1010.100(t) includes gaming establishments with gross annual gaming revenue greater than $1 million that are licensed or authorized to do business as casinos or card clubs in the United States, whether under the laws of a State, territory or possession[4] of the United States, or under the Indian Gaming Regulatory Act (IGRA)[5] or other Federal, State, or tribal law or arrangement affecting Indian lands.[6] For example, tribal gaming establishments that offer slot machines, video lottery terminals, or table games and that have gross annual gaming revenue in excess of $1 million are subject to FinCEN's regulatory requirements.[7] The definition applies to both land-based and riverboat operations. Card clubs generally are subject to the same rules as casinos, unless a different treatment for card clubs is explicitly stated in FinCEN's regulations.[8]

In addition, 31 CFR § 1021.320 requires casinos and card clubs to report suspicious transactions (or patterns of transactions) conducted or attempted by, at or through the gaming establishment.[9] This requirement took effect on March 25, 2003. Since October 1997, the Nevada Gaming Commission had required gaming establishments licensed in Nevada to file reports of suspicious transactions under Regulation 6A. On March 20, 2003, prior to the effective date for 31 CFR § 1021.320, the Nevada Gaming Commission removed from Regulation 6A requirements related to the reporting of suspicious transactions. Since April 1, 2003, casinos and card clubs in Nevada and other jurisdictions have been required to report suspicious transactions on FinCEN Form 102, Suspicious Activity Report by Casinos and Card Clubs (SAR-C).

---

4. Territories and possessions include the Commonwealth of Puerto Rico, St. Croix (U.S. Virgin Islands), and Tinian (Northern Mariana Islands). See 31 CFR § 1010.100(zz).

5. The Indian Gaming Regulatory Act is codified at 25 U.S.C. § 2701 et seq.

6. See 31 CFR §§ 1010.100(t)(5) and (6).

7. Tribal gaming establishments that offer only Class I gaming are not required to report suspicious transactions and are not financial institutions under 31 CFR § 103.100(t). See 31 U.S.C. §§ 5312(2)(x)(ii) and 5318(g)(1). Class I gaming is defined in the Indian Gaming Regulatory Act as social games played solely for prizes of minimal value or traditional forms of Indian gaming engaged in by individuals as part of, or in connection with, tribal ceremonies or celebrations. See 25 U.S.C. § 2703(b).

8. See 31 CFR § 1010.100(t)(5)(iii).

9. The rule includes a threshold of $5,000 in funds or other assets and permits the voluntary filing of SAR-Cs. See 31 CFR § 1021.320(a).

SAR-Cs serve as a valuable tool to help law enforcement deter and track illicit activity. Gaming establishments subject to FinCEN regulations must also submit Currency Transaction Report by Casinos (CTRC) filings on cash transactions exceeding $10,000. To ensure that these reports also have value for investigators, FinCEN in 2007 excluded from CTRC reporting jackpots from slot machines and certain other types of transactions that posed little risk of money laundering or tax evasion.[10]

Under delegated authority, the Internal Revenue Service (IRS) examines casinos and card clubs, including those that operate in tribal jurisdictions, for compliance with FinCEN's regulations. If the IRS identifies deficiencies, it refers the matter to FinCEN for disposition, including consideration of civil money penalties and remedial actions.[11]

---

10. The number of CTRC filings declined 35 percent in the 12 months before and after the regulatory change. See http://www.fincen.gov/news_room/rp/files/CasinoIndustryCTRFilings.pdf.

11. FinCEN has assessed civil money penalties against several casinos for violations of the BSA and implementing regulations. The latest enforcement action related to a tribal casino in Minnesota. See http://www.fincen.gov/news_room/nr/html/20110421.html

Methodology

FinCEN analysts conducted BSA database research to identify distinct SAR-C filings made between January 1, 2004, and June 30, 2011. This method identified 74,816 unique SAR-Cs that form the basis for the statistical analyses in this report, unless otherwise specified. Analysts derived statistics from the items reported on all SAR-Cs filed.

To learn more about the kinds of suspicious activities reported, analysts reviewed the narratives of a random sample of 3,916 SAR-Cs to ascertain the types of transactions, activities, or behaviors that raised red flags and prompted filers to submit the SAR-Cs. Of the reports reviewed, filers submitted 2,864 from January 2004 through 2008, and the remainder from January 2009 through June 30, 2011. The sample size provides a confidence level of 95 percent with a confidence interval of plus or minus 3 percent.

Research and Analysis

Filing Volume and Suspicious Activity Dollar Amounts

From January 1, 2004 through June 30, 2011, casinos and card clubs filed nearly 75,000 SAR-Cs reporting dollar amounts totaling approximately $1.8 billion. The number of monthly filings fluctuated and did not appear to be seasonal. Annual filings increased year-to-year, and doubled from 2004 to 2009. The volume of filings in the first half of 2011 exceeded the number filed in the first half of 2010 and was on track to continue the pattern of yearly increases.

Annual suspicious activity dollar amounts fluctuated, with decreases in 2005 and 2008. The greatest annual increase in both filings and reported activity dollar amounts occurred in 2007, when the volume of SAR-Cs increased by 37 percent and reported amounts jumped by 70 percent.

Figure 1 shows monthly and yearly SAR-C filings. Figure 2 depicts annual filing changes. Figure 3 summarizes annual filings and suspicious activity dollar amounts.

Figure 1

Monthly and Annual Filings SAR-Cs Filed January 1, 2004 - June 30, 2011								
	2004	*2005*	*2006*	*2007*	*2008*	*2009*	*2010*	*2011*	*Total*
January	498	469	420	752	967	1,016	1,118	1,144	6,384
February	539	454	516	659	966	814	1,157	1,173	6,278
March	438	527	629	910	802	980	1,015	1,397	6,698
April	516	554	459	868	765	801	1,097	1,569	6,629
May	446	512	654	740	1,065	1,132	1,149	1,553	7,251
June	407	486	732	821	812	917	1,127	1,491	6,793
July	558	533	591	767	842	1,039	867	N/A	5,197
August	431	432	543	978	1,167	1,135	1,496	N/A	6,182
September	491	513	682	823	865	961	1,149	N/A	5,484
October	590	433	653	790	1,140	1,099	1,391	N/A	6,096
November	467	447	580	1,161	808	1,125	1,116	N/A	5,704
December	581	712	811	674	963	1,075	1,304	N/A	6,120
Total	5,962	6,072	7,270	9,943	11,162	12,094	13,986	8,327	74,816

Figure 2

NOTE: Analysts calculated the percentage change from 2010 to 2011 based on filings in the first 6 months of each year.

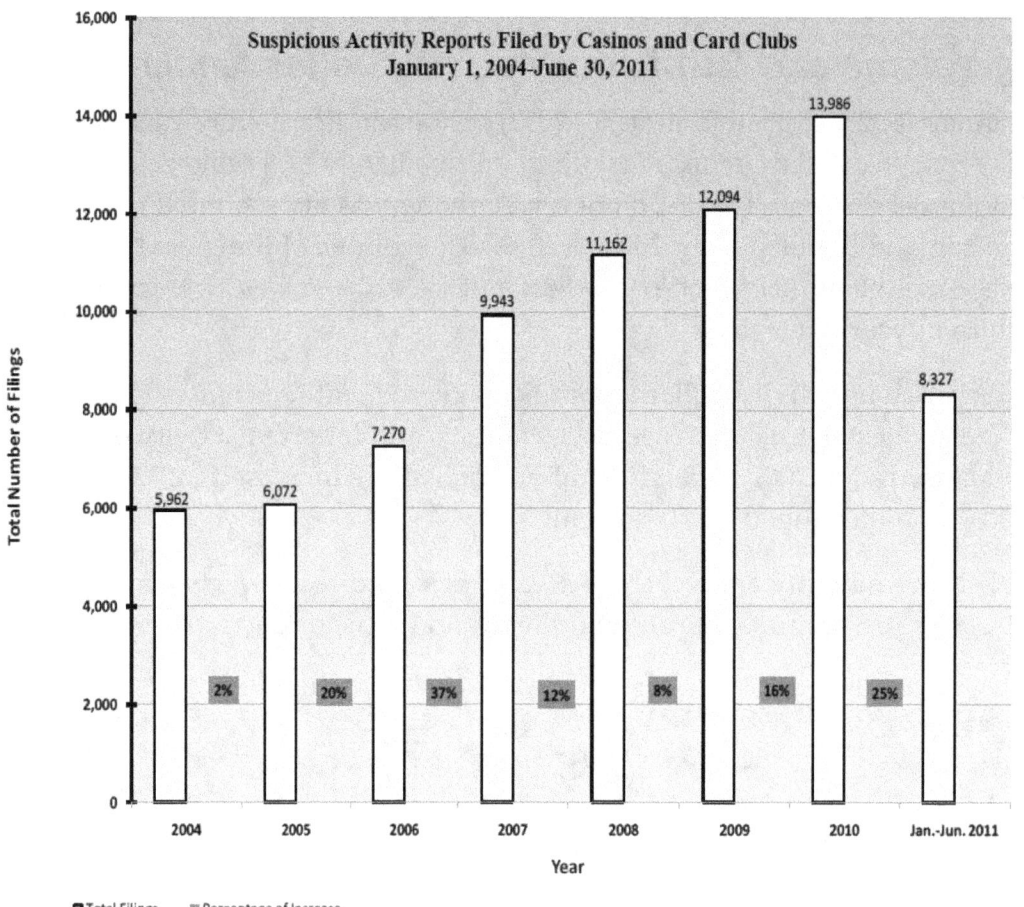

Figure 3

Filing Year	# of Filings	% of Total SAR-C Filings Over Period of Analysis	% Change in Filings From Previous Year	Total Amount[12]	% of 2004 to 2011 Total $ Amount	% Change in $ Amount From Previous Year
Annual Filings and Reported Suspicious Activity Dollar Amounts SAR-Cs Filed January 1, 2004 - June 30, 2011						
2004[13]	5,962	8%	-	$114,066,941	6%	<1%
2005	6,072	8%	2%	$107,979,564	6%	-5%
2006	7,270	10%	20%	$164,717,181	9%	53%
2007	9,943	13%	37%	$279,475,643	16%	70%
2008	11,162	15%	12%	$254,867,024	14%	-9%
2009	12,094	16%	8%	$312,976,965	18%	23%
2010	13,986	19%	16%	$306,545,007	17%	2%
2011[14]	8,327	11%	25%	$229,831,317	13%	<1%
Total	74,816	100%		$1,770,459,642	100%	

From 2004 to 2010, the number of filings consistently increased by a minimum of 2 percent per year. However, reported dollar amounts decreased from 2004 to 2005, and again from 2007 to 2008, while the number of filings continued to increase. Based on total filings, the average dollar amount per filing was $23,664, and the median and mode were both $10,000.

---

12. Some SAR-C filings include suspicious activity dollar amounts previously reported on other SAR-C filings. Totals shown represent all reported amounts, including those reported in previous filings.

13. In 2004, a casino reported erroneous suspicious activity dollar amounts for 27 SAR-Cs totaling $663,000,000 that should have been reported as $663,000. The 2004 dollar amount has been adjusted downward to correct this error.

14. Analysts calculated the percentage change in filings for 2011 by comparing the volume of filings in the first half of the year to the number filed in the first half of 2010.

Types of Gaming institutions

Three types of gaming establishments are required to file SAR-Cs: state-licensed casinos, tribal casinos, and card clubs. In the past, the majority of casinos were state licensed, but the number of casinos owned and/or operated by Indian tribes has grown significantly in the past two decades. Tribal jurisdictions are sovereign vis-à-vis the states, which have only limited authority to regulate gaming activities in tribal jurisdictions. The National Indian Gaming Commission, an agency of the federal government, regulates tribal gaming. However, the Indian Gaming Regulatory Act requires the negotiation of Tribal-State compacts,[15] and these arrangements may address, among other matters, how gaming activities in tribal jurisdictions are licensed or regulated.[16]

Both state-licensed and tribal casinos typically offer games where customers essentially bet against the casino or "house." Examples of such games are blackjack, roulette, slot machines, bingo, and keno. Casinos also offer customers a variety of financial services, including maintaining accounts, accepting deposits into these accounts, issuing credit and receiving payments on credit, cashing checks, issuing casino checks, sending and receiving wire transfers, and exchanging currency. Many financial transactions take place at the "cage" or casino bank. (See glossary of casino terms on page 24.) Financial transactions also occur at casino gaming areas, where customers can buy tokens for slot machines or chips for table games.

Card clubs, otherwise known as card rooms, operate much like casinos except that their customers do not bet against "the house." Instead, card clubs provide tables, dealers, and other services to players who gamble against one another in games such as poker. The income of a card room comes from a combination of fees charged for each hand dealt, seat rental fees, and/or a percentage of each "pot." Card clubs offer

---

15. See 25 U.S.C. 2710(d)(3)(A). The requirement to negotiate Tribal-State compacts applies only to Class III gaming. See 25 U.S.C. 2710(d)(1). Class II gaming is regulated exclusively by the National Indian Gaming Commission and functions of tribal government. See 25 U.S.C. §§ 2710(a)(2) and (b). The federal government has no jurisdiction over Class I gaming, which is regulated exclusively by functions of tribal government. See 25 U.S.C. § 2710(a)(1). Slot machines, video lottery terminals, and house-banked table games would qualify as Class III gaming under the Indian Gaming Regulatory Act. See 25 U.S.C. § 2703(8). Bingo and related games, including pull tabs, lotto, punch boards, tip jars, instant bingo and some card games, would qualify as Class II gaming under the Indian Gaming Regulatory Act. See 25 U.S.C. § 2703(7).

16. See 25 U.S.C. 2710(d)(3)(C).

many of the same financial services as traditional casinos. Like casinos, card clubs may maintain a cage where cashiers conduct financial transactions. However, unlike casinos, card clubs rarely extend credit to customers.

State-licensed casinos submitted 70 percent of total SAR-C filings, tribal casinos 26 percent, and card clubs 2 percent. Other types of filers, such as racinos (combinations of race tracks and casinos) and casino cruise ships, filed the remainder. The following is a breakdown of filings by type of gaming institution.[17]

Figure 4

Type of Gaming Institution Filer[18] SAR-Cs Filed January 1, 2004 - June 30, 2011				
Type of Filer	*# of Filings*	*% of Filings*	*Suspicious Activity Amount*	*% of Total Amount*
State Licensed	52,724	70%	$1,422,812,519	80%
Tribal Licensed	19,090	26%	$290,799,047	16%
Card Club	1,387	2%	$42,137,911	2%
Other	121	<1%	$3,772,947	<1%
Unspecified	1,243	2%	$13,874,241	1%

Filings Categorized by State[19]

New Jersey casinos submitted 22 percent of all filings and ranked first in filing volume. Nevada casinos were second, with 19 percent of filings. Casinos in California and Mississippi, which each submitted 7 percent of filings, were the next most frequent filers.

Based on suspicious activity dollar amount, Nevada casinos ranked first, reporting approximately 44 percent of the total amount. New Jersey filers reported 17 percent of the total activity amount, while casinos in California and Mississippi each reported 4 percent.

Nine of the top 10 filing states by volume of reports also ranked in the top 10 by transaction dollar amounts. The exceptions were Connecticut, 7th highest by volume but not among the top 10 by dollar amount, and Puerto Rico, 9th by dollar amount but not among the top 10 by volume. The top 10 filing states accounted for 83 percent of total filings and 91 percent of transaction amounts.

---

17. Field 39 in Part IV of the SAR-C elicits information on the type of gaming institution. A filer may report one or more types of gaming institution in a SAR-C, where applicable. As a result, columns do not total 100 percent.

18. Some filers listed multiple casino types. Therefore the filings may be counted in more than one category.

19. For comparison purposes, the commonwealth of Puerto Rico was included in the analysis of state filers.

Figures 5 and 6 show the top 10 states by filing volume and transaction amounts.

Figure 5

Top 10 States by Number of Filings		
SAR-Cs Filed January 1, 2004 - June 30, 2011		
Filer State	*# of Filings*	*% of All Filings*
New Jersey	16,382	22%
Nevada	14,169	19%
Louisiana	5,331	7%
California	4,962	7%
Mississippi	4,555	6%
Oklahoma	4,382	6%
Connecticut	3,582	5%
Indiana	2,965	4%
Illinois	2,869	4%
Michigan	2,088	3%
Total	61,285	83%

Figure 6

Top 10 States by Suspicious Activity Dollar Amount		
SAR-Cs Filed January 1, 2004 - June 30, 2011		
Filer State	*Suspicious Activity Amount*	*% of Total Amount*
Nevada	$782,158,563	44%
New Jersey	$293,617,110	17%
California	$121,157,676	7%
Mississippi	$115,443,801	7%
Oklahoma	$66,610,926	4%
Louisiana	$64,632,058	4%
Illinois	$55,791,358	3%
Indiana	$44,647,863	3%
Puerto Rico	$22,973,974	1%
Michigan	$17,244,262	1%
Total	$1,584,277,591	91%

The following map depicts filing volumes for all states.   Appendix A shows yearly filings and suspicious activity amounts for all states.

SAR-Cs Filed January 1, 2004 - June 30, 2011

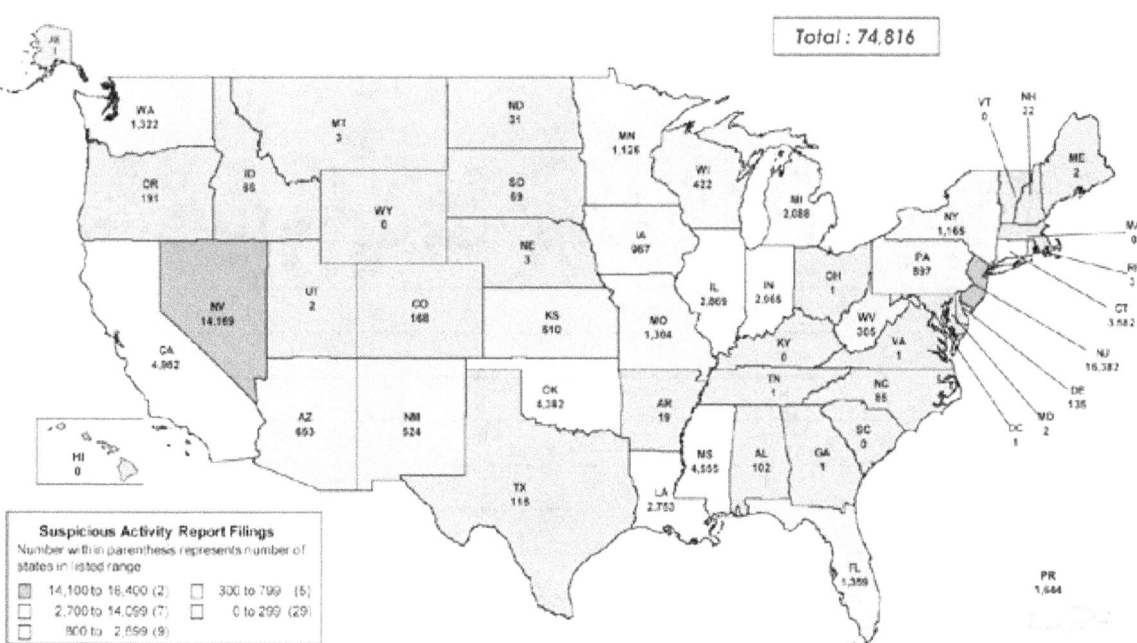

Filers

The information in this section applies only to SAR-Cs filed January 1, 2009 - June 30, 2011. Please see page 28 for filer data from January 1, 2004 – June 30, 2011. *(Rev. April 27, 2012)*

More than 700 different filers submitted SAR-Cs. State-licensed casinos and tribal casinos submitted the bulk of filings, while card clubs submitted the least.[20] Nevertheless, one tribal casino and one card club were among the top 10 filers, which submitted 12 percent of all filings. These filers are listed by type in Figure 7.

Figure 7

Top 10 Filers and Number of Filings	
SAR-Cs Filed January 1, 2009 - June 30, 2011	
Filer Type	**Number of Filings**
State Licensed Casino	1,483
State Licensed Casino	1,261
Tribal Casino	972
State Licensed Casino	905
Card Club	896
State Licensed Casino	818
State Licensed Casino	783
State Licensed Casino	739
State Licensed Casino	688
State Licensed Casino	678

---

20. Filing institution counts are derived from the reported Employer Identification Number (EIN). Four percent of filings omitted the filer EIN entirely or provided clearly incorrect information. Calculations herein do not take these into account.

Interestingly, no casinos located in Nevada ranked among the top 10 by number of filings. However, Nevada casinos reported significantly larger suspicious activity amounts per filing than did casinos in other parts of the county. Figure 8 shows the 10 largest filers by type of gaming institution and dollar amount reported. Six of these filers are from Nevada.

Figure 8

Top 10 Filers by Suspicious Activity Dollar Amount SAR-Cs Filed January 1, 2009 – June 30, 2011			
Filer Type	Number of Filings	Total Suspicious Activity Dollar Amount Reported	Average Dollar Amount per Filing
State Licensed Casino	549	$220,873,376	$402,319
State Licensed Casino	458	$87,827,756	$191,763
State Licensed Casino	1,483	$39,728,582	$26,789
State Licensed Casino	548	$33,872,602	$61,811
State Licensed Casino	570	$31,543,227	$55,338
State Licensed Casino	346	$28,557,903	$82,537
State Licensed Casino	818	$28,278,977	$34,570
Card Club	896	$23,215,494	$25,910
State Licensed Casino	346	$21,102,919	$60,991
State Licensed Casino	251	$20,651,945	$82,278

Characterizations of Suspicious Activity

Types of suspicious activities most frequently reported on SAR-Cs were "Structuring" (41 percent), "Minimal Gaming with Large Transactions" (22 percent), and "Other" (23 percent).[21] Figures 9 and 10 show filings by suspicious activity type. For most types of activities reported, the upward trend over the period of the study was generally consistent with the growth in volume of filings. Two notable exceptions that showed especially large increases from the first to the last full year of the study were "Unusual Use of Negotiable Instruments (Checks)" and "Unusual Use of Counter Checks or Markers."

---

21. Statistics are based on filer data in Field 26 of the SAR-C. Columns in Figure 9 do not equal annual totals because some SAR-Cs showed multiple suspicious activity types and others did not report the type of suspicious activity.

Figure 9

Types of Suspicious Activity Reported SAR-Cs Filed January 1, 2004 – June 30, 2011									
	Number of Filings								
	2004	*2005*	*2006*	*2007*	*2008*	*2009*	*2010*	*2011*	*Total*
Bribery/gratuity	14	15	22	32	28	32	20	15	178
Check fraud (includes counterfeit)	203	114	246	344	336	495	614	234	2,586
Credit/debit card fraud (includes counterfeit)	90	17	51	68	84	144	208	89	751
Embezzlement/ Theft	23	21	32	36	66	108	80	33	399
Large currency exchange(s)	319	322	343	381	464	577	670	373	3,449
Minimal gaming with large transactions	1,116	1,149	1,263	2,197	2,655	2,822	3,160	1,920	16,282
Misuse of position	11	9	15	26	43	28	22	20	174
Money laundering	320	324	277	373	431	523	613	415	3,276
No apparent business or lawful purpose	360	405	411	455	732	809	758	586	4,516
Structuring	2,537	2,568	2,661	3,533	4,588	4,811	6,019	3,768	30,485
Unusual use of negotiable instruments (checks)	74	94	202	306	304	370	407	201	1,958
Use of multiple credit or deposit accounts	18	10	11	15	8	25	18	9	114
Unusual use of wire transfers	74	50	45	78	83	78	91	98	597
Unusual use of counter checks or markers	48	129	269	401	450	405	522	225	2,449
False or conflicting ID(s)	452	425	717	1,196	1,183	1,257	1,141	540	6,911
Terrorist financing	1	1	4	12	3	2	1	5	29
Other	1,455	1,639	2,310	2,467	2,463	2,487	2,523	1,490	16,834

Figure 10

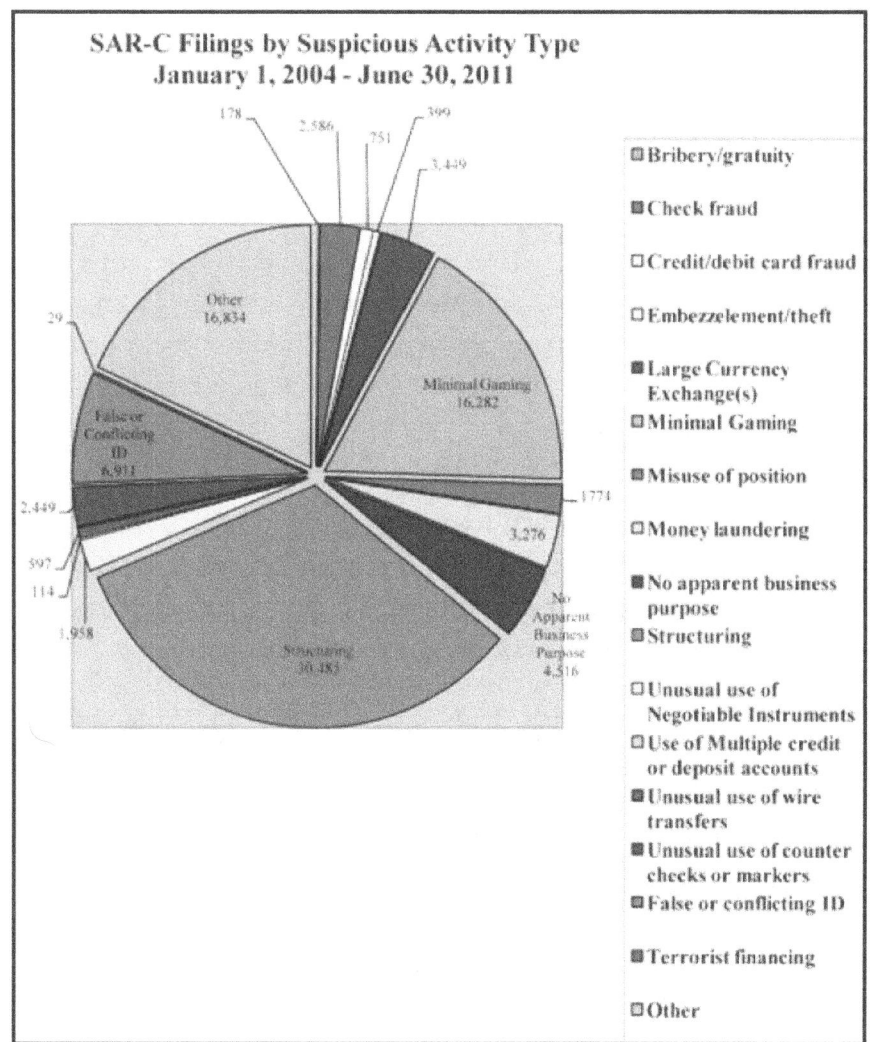

Activities Described in SAR-C Narratives

FinCEN reviewed the narratives of 3,916 randomly selected SAR-C reports and categorized the types of transactions, activities, or behaviors that prompted the filings.[22] This section provides examples of the types of activity frequently reported in the narratives. The glossary on page 24 defines the casino-related terms used in this section.

Structuring

Nearly 64 percent of the sampled narratives described evidence of structuring or apparent attempts to avoid currency transaction reporting requirements.[23] This percentage was significantly higher than the 41 percent of filings that characterized the activity as structuring in Field 26 of the SAR-C form.[24]

The most frequently reported structuring activity involved patron attempts to reduce the dollar amount received from chip redemptions, apparently to avoid a CTR-C filing. Casinos often detected these activities at the time of redemption through pit/cashier communication, cashier familiarity with the patron, or surveillance. Suspicious activities that were not identified at the time of the transaction were later identified through internal reviews of Multiple Transaction Log (MTL) or player rating records. Key structuring activities that casinos reported included the following patron activities:

---

22. The percentages in this section were determined on the basis of FinCEN analyst reviews of SAR-C narratives, and not the type of suspicious activity selected in Field 26 of the SAR-C. As a result, the percentages in this section differ from those in previous sections.

23. Casinos and card clubs must file Form 103 (Currency Transaction Report by Casinos) for each transaction involving either currency received (Cash In) or currency disbursed (Cash Out) of more than $10,000 in a gaming day. A gaming day is the normal business day of the casino by which it keeps its books and records for business, accounting, and tax purposes. Multiple transactions must be treated as a single transaction if the casino has knowledge that: (a) they are made by or on behalf of the same person, and (b) they result in either Cash In or Cash Out by the casino totaling more than $10,000 during any one gaming day. See 31 CFR § 1021.311.

24. Some filers may not have selected "structuring" as the activity type in Field 26 because they did not interpret the reported activity as "structuring."

- Reducing the number of chips or tokens to be cashed out at a cage when asked to provide identification or a Social Security Number (SSN), when the cash out was over $10,000, or when a subject had previously cashed out chips or tokens and the additional cash out would exceed $10,000 in a gaming day. This was the most frequently reported structuring activity.

- Reducing the amount of cash buy-ins at gaming tables to avoid providing identification or an SSN.

- Using agents to cash out chips. Casino employees observed individuals handing chips to associates (agents) to be redeemed on behalf of the playing customer. After cashing out, the agents often passed the cash to the individual who originally handed over the chips. Although some of the narratives identified the names of all the individuals involved, most listed only one individual in the SAR-C subject field, usually the person who originally handed over the chips. The agents were often unidentified because transaction amounts were below reporting thresholds and did not require patrons to provide identification, or because agent interactions with the chip owners took place after transactions were complete. However, filers that did identify agents often named the individual who originally handed over the chips as the subject and listed agents in the narrative.

- Cashing out chips, tickets, and/or tokens multiple times a day, at different times, or at different windows/cages.

- Requesting jackpot winnings exceeding $10,000 to be paid in two or three payments. In some cases, winnings were placed on deposit and withdrawn in cash amounts under the currency transaction reporting threshold.

- Wiring funds into front money accounts and withdrawing those funds, in cash, in smaller increments to avoid conducting one large-dollar reportable transaction.

- Repaying outstanding balances with structured cash payments, apparently to avoid a reportable transaction.

- Purchasing chips with cash just under the reporting threshold and then purchasing additional chips at the table, again with cash.

- Placing bets at multiple sportsbooks, usually at related properties, in an attempt to structure bets that in the aggregate would exceed the reporting threshold. Placing bets at multiple properties may also conceal aggregated winnings over the reporting threshold.

Minimal or No Play

About 19 percent of the sampled narratives reported patrons conducting transactions that involved minimal or no play.[25] Casinos reported the following types of activities:

- Cashing out chips when the casino had no record of the individual having bought or played with chips.[26]

- Buying chips with cash, casino credit, credit card advances, wired funds, or funds withdrawn from safekeeping accounts, and then playing minimally or not playing at all. Some subjects cashed out chips while others left the casino with unredeemed chips.

- Receiving wired funds into a casino front money account and then requesting that the funds be wired to a bank account without playing.

- Frequently depositing money orders or casino checks from other casinos into front money accounts, buying in and playing minimally, or not playing and then cashing out through issuance of a casino check.

False or Invalid Identification

Two percent of the sampled narratives reported subjects misusing or attempting to misuse identification by providing false, expired, stolen or altered personal identifiers or identification credentials, mainly SSNs and drivers' licenses. Winnings from gambling are subject to federal, and in some cases, state taxes, and casinos report customer winnings above specified amounts to the IRS. Casinos often identified false SSNs when patrons provided multiple SSNs, or when casinos received alerts about the mismatch from the IRS.

---

25. Minimal casino play most commonly refers to situations in which individuals exchange large amounts of currency for casino chips, gamble for a short period of time, either lose a nominal amount of money or make small bets in comparison to the buy-in, and then immediately cash out their chips. See Suspicious Activity Report Filings within the Casino and Card Clubs Industries, *SAR Activity Review, Trends, Tips and Issues, Issue 8*, April 2005, page 13 at http://www.fincen.gov/news_room/rp/files/sar_tti_17.pdf.

26. Casino records about a patron may be limited unless the individual participates in a player rating system, for which casinos collect personally identifiable information. Without this information, casinos may find it difficult to associate chip purchases, chip redemptions, winnings and losses with patrons unless transactions reach amounts that require identification.

Fraud Against the Casino Involving Checks and Other Instruments

One percent of the sampled narratives indicated fraud or attempted fraud against the casino through activities involving checks, counterfeit currency, or misuse of player's club points. Examples include the following:

- Customers secured markers with personal checks that were returned unpaid, either because the account held insufficient funds or because the depository institution had previously closed the account.

- Patrons negotiated or attempted to negotiate stolen, forged, or altered checks.

- Patrons attempted to pass counterfeit bills.

- A few SAR-Cs reported that casino patrons used their player club points to purchase significant amounts of merchandise at independently owned and operated retail stores on casino premises. Employees of the retail stores or third parties assisted the patrons in converting the merchandise into cash. In some instances, the casino suspected that no merchandise was actually purchased. Instead, filers said the subjects created sham paper sale transactions and paid cash directly to the patrons for the player club points. The retail stores in turn received monetary reimbursement from the casino for sales involving the use of player club points.

"Other" Activities

Filers indicated "other" in Field 26 of the SAR-C as the second largest characterization of suspicious activity. In some cases, filers selected "other" but described in the narrative activities that appeared to fall within one or more of the categories listed on the form, such as structuring. Narrative descriptions of activity accurately identified as "other" often included allegations that patrons or employees displayed unusual behavior or that employees violated the casino's internal policies. Examples include:

- Customers repeatedly inquired about the CTR-C reporting requirements, and whether their buy-ins and/or cash-outs had reached the reporting threshold. In answering their inquiries, most casino employees reportedly described CTR-C requirements or provided the patrons with an information card about CTR-C filing, and refused to answer questions about individual thresholds.

- A high-stakes player frequently wired funds via depository institutions to the front money account of another high-stakes customer.

- Customers used markers as casino loans by requesting advances on credit through markers, often at gaming tables, then not playing or playing minimally.

- Customers using player rating accounts recorded gaming history on each other's accounts, possibly to conceal wins and losses by each customer.

- Surveillance determined that the person attempting to claim a slot jackpot was not the actual jackpot winner. Filers did not always ascertain if the patrons attempting to claim the jackpots were associates of the actual winner.

- Patrons wagered higher amounts than their occupations appeared able to support.

- A few casino employees assisted customers by failing to log patrons' multiple currency transactions into the casinos' Multiple Transaction Logs.[27]

Money Laundering/ Exchanging Bills

Less than 1 percent of the filings described money laundering in their narratives. Of these, filers described the following situations in which patrons exchanged small denomination for large denomination bills, reportedly in attempts to launder the proceeds of criminal activity.

- Patrons inserted large numbers of small denomination bills into casino gaming machines with little or no play in order to exchange small bills for casino tokens. Patrons then redeemed the casino tokens for large bills.

- Patrons used small bills to buy in at gaming tables, received large denomination chips, and redeemed those chips with little or no play for large denomination bills.

---

27. Reports of suspected insider abuse and collusion provide valuable information for law enforcement. FinCEN Advisory 2009-A003, Structuring by Casino Patrons and Personnel, provides specific guidance for casinos. See http://www.fincen.gov/statutes_regs/guidance/pdf/fin-2009-a003.pdf.

Summary

FinCEN's analysis indicates that filings of SAR-Cs by casinos and card club grew every year from 2004 to 2010, a period when gaming activities continued to expand. Based on total filings, the average dollar amount of suspicious activity reported per filing was $23,664, and the median was $10,000. Some casinos reported much higher averages: reports by one casino averaged $402,319. Over the study period, the total amount of suspicious activity reported was $1.77 billion.

The types of activities described most frequently in SAR-C narratives were suspected structuring and financial transactions with minimal or no gaming activity. In SAR-Cs where the casino or card club indicated "other" as the characterization of suspicious activity, narratives often included allegations that patrons or employees displayed unusual behavior or violated casino policies. A smaller number of narratives reported use of false or invalid identification, fraud against the casino involving checks or other instruments, and unusual transactions indicative of money laundering. Reports of these activities generally reflected FinCEN's guidance concerning red flags for casinos and card clubs.[28]

---

28. See Recognizing Suspicious Activity—Red Flags for Casinos and Card Clubs at
   http://www.fincen.gov/statutes_regs/guidance/pdf/fin-2008-g007.pdf.

Glossary of Casino Terms[29]

- **Casino Cage:** A secure work area within a casino that houses cashiers and storage facilities for cash, chips, tokens, and credit documents. Cashiers at the cage conduct transactions with customers and other casino areas.

- **Front Money:** Money deposited by a customer into a personal casino account with a cage cashier. The customer can later withdraw the front money at gaming tables or at the cage in the form of chips, currency, casino check, or wire transfer.

- **Marker or Counter Check:** Credit extended to a customer in exchange for chips, tokens, or currency. The marker or counter check is intended for use in gambling.

- **Multiple Transaction Log:** Casino and card club documents used to record and keep track of customer currency transaction activity above a given dollar threshold. Many casinos and card clubs maintain multiple transaction logs for pit and cage (including slot booth) transactions, sometimes pursuant to state, local, or tribal gaming laws, or within the ordinary course of business.

- **Player Club Points:** Many casinos award "club points" based on how much customers bet and how often they play. Patrons can redeem these club points for goods and services at restaurants, retail shops, or hotels.

- **Player Rating Card:** A card used in a casino pit to keep track of a player's activity at a single gaming table for purposes of determining if a player is entitled to receive complimentary services ("comps"). Each time a rated player begins gambling at a table, designated casino employees who monitor customer's play prepare a "player rating card," also known as a "rating card" or "rating slip."

- **Player Rating:** Casinos use a variety of methods to award complimentary services to attract and retain their customers. The most common method is based on theoretical win, the amount a casino expects to win from a particular customer. It is calculated using a number of factors, including the length of time the gambler plays.

---

29. Definitions were assembled from a variety of sources, including internal FinCEN documents, the IRS examination manual for casinos (see http://www.irs.gov/irm/part4/irm_04-026-009.html), and http://www.americangaming.org/files/aga/uploads/docs/sos/aga-sos-2011.pdf

- **Pit:** An area of a casino or card club floor that contains gaming tables. Each pit contains several gaming tables organized by game type. Each pit is under the supervision of a single floor supervisor (or "pit boss"). Customers can buy chips and conduct other transactions at the pit.

- **Sportsbook:** A place where individuals can wager on various sports competitions, such as golf, football, basketball, baseball, boxing, and horse racing. Three states currently authorize legal betting on sporting events through casinos (Nevada), the state lottery (Oregon), or race tracks (Delaware).

- **Surveillance:** Casinos routinely use extensive surveillance systems including video cameras, monitors, recorders, video printers, switches, selectors and other ancillary equipment to observe and record activities at the gaming establishment. Casinos often identify individuals conducting unusual, suspicious or potentially criminal financial transactions through surveillance.

Appendix A: Annual SAR-C Filings by State[30]

STATE/ TERRITORY	2004	2005	2006	2007	2008	2009	2010	2011[31]	Total Filings	Dollar Amount
Alabama	-	1	-	-	2	9	44	46	102	$861,836
Alaska	-	-	-	-	-	1	-	-	1	$2,000
Arizona	41	37	75	94	101	69	126	120	663	$11,043,907
Arkansas	-	-	-	1	6	8	4	-	19	$147,041
California	264	285	452	596	811	807	1147	600	4,962	$121,157,676
Colorado	9	7	14	12	18	26	56	26	168	$1,379,927
Connecticut	265	394	552	624	548	464	523	212	3,582	$66,610,926
Delaware	11	15	9	12	5	2	46	35	135	$1,328,739
District Of Columbia	-	-	-	-	-	1	-	-	1	$20
Florida	25	40	128	224	171	255	305	211	1359	$19,232,049
Georgia	-	-	1	-	-	-	-	-	1	$10,000
Idaho	5	9	4	17	7	11	12	1	66	$2,976,511
Illinois	300	245	323	508	416	418	446	213	2,869	$55,791,358
Indiana	378	315	367	485	348	394	460	218	2,965	$44,647,863
Iowa	122	116	108	153	142	121	103	102	967	$10,004,464
Kansas	21	20	36	60	186	64	61	62	510	$8,020,420
Louisiana	273	419	721	663	677	914	1090	574	2,753	$64,632,058
Maine	-	-	-	-	-	2	-	-	2	$13,000
Maryland	-	-	1	-	-	-	-	1	2	$11,450
Michigan	225	144	172	176	207	316	577	271	2,088	$17,244,262
Minnesota	60	56	102	163	215	182	222	126	1,126	$13,380,826
Mississippi	652	449	348	435	570	596	977	528	4,555	$115,443,801
Missouri	73	104	91	72	93	305	360	206	1304	$13,005,177

30. Statistics are based on filer state data in Field 37 of the SAR-C form. Figures for states without covered gaming operations may stem from data processing errors or filings not required by BSA regulations.

31. 2011 filings are through June 30.

Montana	-	-	-	-	2	1	-	-	3	$33,234
Nebraska	-	-	1	-	-	1	1	-	3	$40,265
Nevada	804	827	921	2,041	2,504	2,810	2,707	1,555	14,169	$782,158,563
New Hampshire	-	-	-	-	-	20	-	2	22	$319,535
New Jersey	1,927	1,993	1,891	2,284	2,596	2,151	2,069	1,471	16,382	$293,617,110
New Mexico	38	47	72	99	54	76	85	53	524	$4,396,353
New York	121	184	125	157	164	160	195	59	1,165	$15,786,702
North Carolina	8	16	23	9	7	9	9	4	85	$736,615
North Dakota	-	5	3	5	3	6	6	3	31	$255,079
Ohio	-	-	-	-	-	-	1	-	1	$5,024
Oklahoma	46	79	458	763	747	897	874	518	4,382	$38,787,898
Oregon	15	16	31	8	18	53	34	16	191	$1,535,406
Pennsylvania	1	-	-	11	30	85	306	464	897	$8,641,052
Puerto Rico	148	54	62	49	128	336	526	341	1644	$22,973,974
Rhode Island	-	1	-	-	-	-	-	2	3	$109,715
South Dakota	2	5	4	4	10	23	14	7	69	$303,192
Tennessee	-	-	-	-	-	1	-	-	1	$13,900
Texas	3	2	5	2	26	41	20	19	118	$702,904
US Virgin Islands	-	-	1	-	1	-	2	-	4	$135,500
Utah	-	-	-	1	-	1	-	-	2	$73,119
Virginia	-	-	-	-	-	-	1	-	1	$3,001
Washington	48	99	72	113	185	262	403	140	1322	$15,382,092
West Virginia	6	11	5	3	62	88	81	49	305	$6,581,005
Wisconsin	35	50	47	53	59	57	63	58	422	$5,970,136
Unknown/ Incorrect State Codes	36	27	45	46	43	51	30	14	292	$4,952,957
	5,962	6,072	7,270	9,943	11,162	12,094	13,986	8,327	74,816	$1,770,459,642

Filer Data *(Added April 27, 2012)*

Figure 11 shows the type of gaming institution and number of reports submitted by the top 10 SAR-C filers from January 1, 2004, through June 30, 2011. Figure 12 lists the 10 filers who reported the largest total dollar amounts of suspicious activity.

Figure 11

Top 10 Filers and Number of Filings SAR-Cs Filed January 1, 2004 – June 30, 2011	
Filer Type	*Number of Filings*
State Licensed Casino	3,076
Tribal Casino	2,433
State Licensed Casino	1,813
State Licensed Casino	1,704
State Licensed Casino	1,628
State Licensed Casino	1,577
State Licensed Casino	1,567
State Licensed Casino	1,370
State Licensed Casino	1,232
State Licensed Casino	1,231

Figure 12

Top 10 Filers by Suspicious Activity Dollar Amount SAR-Cs Filed January 1, 2004 – June 30, 2011			
Filer Type	*Number of Filings*	*Total Suspicious Activity Dollar Amount Reported*	*Average Dollar Amount per Filing*
State Licensed Casino	984	$197,408,901	$200,619
State Licensed Casino	646	$148,155,293	$229,343
State Licensed Casino	994	$67,529,075	$21,719
State Licensed Casino	3,076	$66,806,143	$67,937
State Licensed Casino	583	$51,455,093	$88,259
Tribal Casino	2,433	$41,584,850	$17,092
State Licensed Casino	739	$37,559,400	$50,825
State Licensed Casino	1,104	$32,572,238	$29,667
State Licensed Casino	1,231	$30,887,399	$25,091
State Licensed Casino	549	$29,256,516	$53,291

www.FinCEN.gov